Table Of Contents

Chapter 2: Retail Businesses 1
Chapter 3: Food and Beverage Industry 1
Chapter 4: Health and Wellness 1
Chapter 5: Professional Services 1
Chapter 6: Creative Industries 1
Chapter 7: Technology and IT Services 1
Chapter 8: Home and Personal Services 1
Chapter 9: Education and Training 1
Chapter 10: List Of Businesses and Services They Need 1
Chapter 11: Conclusion and Next Steps 1
Chapter 1: Introduction to Side Hustles 1

In a nutshell this book is about providing services and/or products to small businesses that can't live without. Some of these businesses may already know they need your services, or they may not. The bottom line of your proposal is you will be providing a convenience to the owner/s and/or adding efficiency to their operations. Increasing their bottom-line profits may be all they care about but adding a convenience may free up some time they can use to focus on building their business as you provide the services in the background.

Maybe hopefully this book will spark some interest and give you some good ideas as you try to figure out your next move in your pursuit to greater income or just freedom to work on your own terms. There's a big list of ideas that you can study for ideas. This list could possibly spark a whole new idea. Whatever the case I wish you best of success in your endeavors.

Chapter 1: Introduction to Side Hustles

The Rise of the Side Hustle

The rise of the side hustle has transformed the landscape of entrepreneurship, allowing individuals to explore personal passions while generating additional income. This trend has been fueled by various factors, including technological advancements, economic fluctuations, and a cultural shift towards valuing flexibility and autonomy. As traditional job security diminishes, more people are seeking alternative avenues to supplement their income, leading to a surge in side businesses that cater to niche markets.

One significant driver of this phenomenon is the accessibility of online platforms. Entrepreneurs can now leverage social media, e-commerce, and freelance marketplaces to launch their side hustles with minimal upfront investment. These platforms enable individuals to showcase their skills and services, connecting them with potential clients who require specific solutions. The digital economy has democratized entrepreneurship, allowing anyone with a viable idea and the determination to succeed to carve out their niche.

Furthermore, the side hustle movement aligns with a growing desire for work-life balance. Many individuals are pursuing side ventures that reflect their passions or hobbies, such as photography, graphic design, or handmade crafts. This approach not only provides financial benefits but also fosters personal fulfillment. Entrepreneurs can turn their interests into profitable enterprises, creating a dual income stream while maintaining their primary job or responsibilities.

As the side hustle culture continues to flourish, small businesses are increasingly recognizing the value of outsourcing services to freelancers and independent contractors. Entrepreneurs seeking side hustle opportunities can focus on providing essential services that small businesses cannot afford to overlook. This includes areas like social media management, website design, content creation, and digital marketing. By offering these services, side hustlers can fill gaps in the market while helping small businesses thrive in an increasingly competitive environment.

In conclusion, the rise of the side hustle represents a significant shift in how individuals approach work, income generation, and personal fulfillment. For aspiring entrepreneurs, this trend presents a wealth of opportunities to develop businesses tailored to their interests and the needs of small enterprises. By identifying and offering essential services that small businesses rely on, individuals can successfully navigate the side hustle landscape, contributing to their financial independence while empowering others in the process.

Understanding Small Business Needs

Understanding the needs of small businesses is crucial for entrepreneurs seeking a side hustle or a new business venture. Small businesses form the backbone of the economy and often face unique challenges that require specific services to thrive. These needs can vary widely based on the industry, size, and market dynamics of each business. By recognizing these requirements, aspiring entrepreneurs can tailor their services to fill gaps in the market, ensuring that they provide valuable support that small businesses cannot do without.

One primary area where small businesses need assistance is in marketing. Many entrepreneurs struggle to effectively promote their products or services, leading to reduced visibility and sales. From social media management to content creation and search engine optimization, there is a significant demand for marketing services that can enhance a small business's reach and engagement. Entrepreneurs can capitalize on this need by offering specialized marketing solutions that cater to the unique voice and mission of each business, helping them connect with their target audience more effectively.

Financial management is another critical need for small businesses, as they often operate on tight budgets and may lack the expertise to handle complex financial tasks. Services such as bookkeeping, tax preparation, and financial consulting are invaluable to small business owners who want to ensure their finances are in order. Entrepreneurs with a background in finance or accounting can find lucrative opportunities by providing these essential services, allowing small business owners to focus on their core operations while maintaining financial health.

Operational efficiency is also a key concern for small businesses. Many entrepreneurs struggle with optimizing their processes, which can lead to wasted resources and reduced profitability. Services that help streamline operations, such as IT support, supply chain management, or project management consulting, can significantly enhance a small business's productivity. Entrepreneurs who can identify inefficiencies and offer solutions will find a receptive market among small business owners looking to improve their operations and achieve better results.

Lastly, small businesses often require support in human resources and compliance. As regulations become more complex, many small business owners feel overwhelmed by the need to manage employee relations, benefits, and legal obligations. Offering HR consulting, recruitment services, or compliance training can address these needs effectively. Entrepreneurs equipped with knowledge in human resources can provide vital support to small businesses, helping them navigate the intricate landscape of workforce management and legal compliance, thereby allowing them to focus on growth and customer satisfaction.

Identifying Your Personal Preferences

Identifying your personal preferences is a crucial first step in selecting a side hustle that aligns with your skills, interests, and lifestyle. This process begins with self-reflection, where you assess what activities bring you joy and satisfaction. Consider what you enjoy doing in your free time and the skills you have developed through your professional and personal experiences. By understanding your passions and strengths, you can create a shortlist of potential side hustle ideas that resonate with you, ensuring your commitment and enthusiasm as you embark on this entrepreneurial journey.

In addition to personal interests, it is essential to evaluate your lifestyle and available resources. Think about how much time you can realistically dedicate to a side hustle while maintaining a balance with your primary job and personal commitments. Consider your financial situation as well; some side hustles require upfront investment, while others may demand minimal initial costs. Aligning your side hustle with your current lifestyle allows you to pursue opportunities that fit seamlessly into your existing routine, reducing stress and increasing the likelihood of success.

Another key aspect of identifying personal preferences is understanding the market demand for various services. Researching the needs of small businesses in your area or online can provide insights into what services are in high demand. For instance, businesses often require assistance with marketing, social media management, bookkeeping, or graphic design. By cross-referencing your skills and passions with the needs of local businesses, you can pinpoint a side hustle that not only excites you but also fulfills a genuine market demand, creating a win-win situation.

Networking with other entrepreneurs and small business owners can also help clarify your preferences and identify viable opportunities. Engaging in conversations and attending local business events can expose you to various services that businesses frequently seek. Through these interactions, you may discover new interests or uncover hidden talents that could inform your side hustle choice. Moreover, building relationships within your community can lead to collaborations and referrals, further enhancing your ability to succeed in your chosen venture.

Finally, don't forget the importance of trial and error in the process of identifying personal preferences. It may take some experimentation to find the right fit for your side hustle. Start small with projects that require minimal commitment and investment. This approach allows you to gauge your interest and aptitude without risking too much time or money. As you gather experiences, refine your focus, and pivot as necessary, you'll be better equipped to identify a side hustle that not only aligns with your personal preferences but also has the potential for sustainable growth.

Chapter 2: Retail Businesses

Essential Services for Retail Stores

Retail stores rely on a variety of essential services to operate efficiently and thrive in a competitive market. These services not only help streamline operations but also enhance customer experiences and drive sales. For entrepreneurs looking to venture into the retail space, understanding these essential services can provide valuable insights into potential side hustle opportunities tailored to their personal preferences and skills.

One of the most critical services for retail stores is inventory management. Effective inventory management systems help businesses keep track of stock levels, manage reordering processes, and reduce excess inventory. Entrepreneurs with a knack for technology can explore opportunities in offering inventory management software solutions or consulting services. This can include training retail staff on best practices, setting up automated tracking systems, or even providing ongoing support to ensure businesses maintain optimal inventory levels.

Another vital service is visual merchandising. The way products are displayed can significantly impact customer engagement and sales. Retailers often need assistance in creating attractive displays that showcase their products effectively. Entrepreneurs with a creative flair can offer visual merchandising services, helping stores design eye-catching layouts and seasonal displays, thus improving foot traffic and encouraging purchases. This service could also extend to digital merchandising for online retailers, focusing on optimizing product presentations on e-commerce platforms.

Marketing and promotional services are equally essential for retail success. With the rise of e-commerce and digital marketing, retail stores must establish a robust online presence to attract customers. Entrepreneurs can consider offering social media management, email marketing, or search engine optimization services specifically tailored to retail businesses. By helping stores develop effective marketing strategies, these entrepreneurs can play a crucial role in driving traffic both online and in-store, ultimately boosting sales.

Lastly, customer service training is a service that many retail stores require to ensure a positive shopping experience. Exceptional customer service can set a store apart from its competitors. Entrepreneurs can develop training programs or workshops designed to equip retail staff with the skills needed to engage with customers effectively, handle inquiries, and resolve complaints. This service not only enhances the customer experience but also contributes to customer loyalty and repeat business, making it a worthwhile investment for any retail operation.

In summary, entrepreneurs looking for side hustle opportunities in the retail sector can explore a range of essential services including inventory management, visual merchandising, marketing, and customer service training. By understanding the needs of retail stores and aligning their services with these demands, aspiring business owners can create successful ventures that cater to the unique challenges faced by retailers today.

Inventory Management Solutions

Effective inventory management is a critical component for small businesses that aim to thrive in competitive markets. Entrepreneurs seeking a side hustle can benefit from understanding various inventory management solutions that cater to their specific needs. These solutions not only streamline operations but also enhance profitability by minimizing excess stock and reducing stockouts. Exploring the right tools and techniques can empower small business owners to make informed decisions about their inventory and improve their overall efficiency.

One popular solution is cloud-based inventory management software, which offers real-time tracking of inventory levels, sales, and orders. With the ability to access data from any location, entrepreneurs can monitor their stock and make adjustments as needed. Many of these platforms come with features such as automated reordering and integration with e-commerce platforms, enabling seamless operations. For side hustlers who may be managing their businesses part-time, these user-friendly tools simplify complex inventory processes and allow for better time management.

In addition to software solutions, small businesses can benefit from adopting inventory management best practices. Techniques such as the Just-In-Time (JIT) inventory system help reduce holding costs by receiving goods only as they are needed in the production process. This approach can be particularly useful for entrepreneurs who may not have the resources to maintain large inventories. By understanding demand patterns and adjusting purchasing strategies accordingly, small business owners can optimize their inventory levels and enhance cash flow.

Another essential aspect of inventory management is adopting a robust categorization system. By organizing products into categories based on sales velocity, profitability, or shelf life, entrepreneurs can quickly identify which items need attention. This method aids in prioritizing restocking efforts and allows for targeted marketing strategies. For those venturing into retail or e-commerce, employing such categorization not only improves inventory accuracy but also supports better customer service, as businesses can fulfill orders more efficiently.

Lastly, training staff in inventory management practices is vital for maintaining an organized and efficient operation. Whether it's a part-time employee or a family member helping out, ensuring that everyone understands the inventory management system can significantly reduce errors and miscommunications. Entrepreneurs should invest time in providing necessary training and resources, as this will lead to a more cohesive team and a smoother operational flow. By leveraging technology, implementing best practices, and fostering a knowledgeable team, small businesses can effectively manage their inventory and position themselves for long-term success.

Point of Sale Systems

Point of Sale (POS) systems are critical tools for small businesses, facilitating transactions and managing sales data efficiently. These systems have evolved significantly from traditional cash registers to sophisticated digital solutions that integrate various functions, making them essential for entrepreneurs looking to establish a side hustle. A reliable POS system not only streamlines the checkout process but also provides valuable insights into sales trends, inventory management, and customer preferences, which can be pivotal for the growth of a small business.

For small businesses, the choice of a POS system can depend on several factors, including the nature of the business, budget constraints, and specific operational needs. Retail stores, for instance, may benefit from systems that manage inventory in real-time, enabling them to track stock levels and reorder products seamlessly. In contrast, service-based businesses like salons or repair shops might prioritize appointment scheduling and customer relationship management features. By understanding the unique requirements of their niche, entrepreneurs can select POS systems that enhance their operational efficiency and customer experience.

The implementation of a POS system can also lead to improved financial management for small businesses. Many modern POS solutions come with integrated accounting features or can sync with popular accounting software, allowing for easier tracking of sales, expenses, and profits. This integration helps entrepreneurs maintain accurate financial records, which is crucial for making informed business decisions. Furthermore, robust reporting tools within these systems can assist in analyzing sales performance, identifying trends, and forecasting future revenue, thereby aiding in strategic planning.

Moreover, the rise of mobile POS systems has opened new opportunities for entrepreneurs in various sectors. These systems enable businesses to accept payments on-the-go, which is particularly advantageous for food trucks, pop-up shops, and outdoor events. Mobile POS solutions often come with features like inventory management and customer engagement tools, allowing entrepreneurs to provide a seamless shopping experience regardless of their location. This adaptability can be a significant advantage for those looking to enter competitive markets or explore unique business ideas.

In conclusion, investing in a suitable POS system is a crucial step for entrepreneurs venturing into small businesses. It not only enhances the efficiency of transactions but also provides essential data that can drive business growth. By evaluating their specific needs and exploring the various options available, entrepreneurs can leverage POS systems to establish a solid foundation for their side hustle, ensuring they have the tools necessary to thrive in their chosen niche.

Marketing and Advertising Strategies

Marketing and advertising strategies are essential for small businesses, especially for entrepreneurs seeking to establish a side hustle. Understanding the target audience and what drives their purchasing decisions is the first step in crafting an effective marketing plan. This involves conducting market research to identify customer demographics, preferences, and behaviors. By gaining insights into the needs of potential customers, entrepreneurs can tailor their services and marketing messages to resonate with their audience, ultimately increasing the likelihood of attracting and retaining clients.

Digital marketing has become a cornerstone for small businesses due to its cost-effectiveness and broad reach. Entrepreneurs can leverage platforms like social media, email marketing, and search engine optimization (SEO) to promote their services. Creating engaging content that showcases expertise and addresses customer pain points can establish credibility and encourage word-of-mouth referrals. Moreover, utilizing targeted ads on platforms like Facebook and Google allows businesses to reach specific demographics, ensuring marketing efforts are efficiently focused on those most likely to convert.

Networking remains a powerful strategy for small businesses. Entrepreneurs should actively participate in local business events, workshops, and online forums to connect with potential clients and other professionals. Building relationships within the community can lead to collaborations, partnerships, and referrals. Additionally, joining industry-specific organizations can provide access to resources and support, enhancing visibility and credibility in the marketplace. Personal connections can significantly influence consumer trust, making networking an invaluable component of any marketing strategy.

Content marketing is another effective approach for small businesses. By creating valuable and informative content, entrepreneurs can position themselves as thought leaders in their industry. This can include blog posts, videos, podcasts, or how-to guides that not only highlight services but also provide solutions to common problems faced by potential clients. Regularly updating content and sharing it across various platforms can drive traffic to a business's website, improve SEO rankings, and engage audiences, leading to increased customer loyalty and retention.

Finally, measuring the effectiveness of marketing and advertising strategies is crucial for continuous improvement. Entrepreneurs should track key performance indicators (KPIs) such as conversion rates, customer acquisition costs, and return on investment (ROI) for different campaigns. By analyzing this data, business owners can identify which strategies are yielding positive results and which may need adjustment. Regular evaluation and adaptation of marketing efforts ensure that small businesses remain competitive and responsive to changing market conditions, ultimately leading to sustained growth and success.

Chapter 3: Food and Beverage Industry

Catering to Food Service Needs

Catering to food service needs presents a diverse and lucrative opportunity for entrepreneurs seeking a side hustle. The food service industry encompasses a broad spectrum of businesses, including restaurants, cafes, food trucks, catering companies, and meal prep services. Each of these establishments has unique demands that can be effectively met by small business owners who understand their specific needs. By recognizing these requirements, entrepreneurs can tailor their services to provide invaluable support, ultimately contributing to the growth and sustainability of food service operations.

One critical area where food service businesses often seek assistance is in supply chain management. Restaurants and catering companies require a steady stream of high-quality ingredients and supplies to operate efficiently. Entrepreneurs can step in by offering services such as inventory management, vendor relations, and logistics support. By establishing partnerships with local farms, food suppliers, and distributors, small business owners can create a streamlined supply chain for food service clients, ensuring they have access to fresh and reliable products. This not only alleviates stress from the business owner but also enhances the overall quality of the culinary offerings.

Marketing and branding are other essential services that food establishments frequently require. In an industry characterized by fierce competition, having a strong brand presence is vital for attracting and retaining customers. Entrepreneurs can provide digital marketing services, including social media management, website design, and search engine optimization tailored specifically for food service businesses. By helping these establishments craft their online presence and develop engaging marketing strategies, entrepreneurs can significantly impact their clients' visibility and success in a crowded market.

Another service that food service businesses often need is staff training and development. From kitchen personnel to front-of-house staff, the effectiveness and professionalism of employees directly influence the customer experience. Entrepreneurs with expertise in hospitality and culinary training can offer workshops, seminars, or even one-on-one coaching sessions to help food service businesses improve their workforce skills. This investment in employee training not only enhances service quality but also fosters a positive work environment, ultimately leading to higher employee retention rates.

Finally, food service businesses are increasingly focused on sustainability and health-conscious practices. Entrepreneurs can cater to this growing trend by providing consulting services in areas such as waste reduction, eco-friendly packaging solutions, and menu planning that emphasizes healthy, locally sourced ingredients. By aligning their services with the values and preferences of modern consumers, entrepreneurs can help food service businesses not only meet regulatory requirements but also appeal to a conscientious customer base. Emphasizing these sustainable practices can set businesses apart in a competitive landscape, making such services highly sought after.

Menu Development and Pricing

Menu development is a critical aspect of establishing a successful side hustle, particularly for entrepreneurs interested in food services, catering, or any business that relies on a defined set of offerings. A well-crafted menu does not merely list items; it reflects the brand identity, appeals to the target audience, and differentiates the business from competitors. Entrepreneurs should begin by identifying their niche and the preferences of their potential customers. This may involve conducting market research, surveying local demand, and analyzing trends in food and beverage preferences. Understanding the local culture and customer behavior is essential to create a menu that resonates with the intended audience.

When developing a menu, entrepreneurs should consider the variety and balance of offerings. A diverse menu can attract a wider customer base, but it is important to ensure that the items complement each other and align with the brand theme. For instance, a health-focused café may include smoothies, salads, and wholesome snacks, while a comfort food eatery might focus on hearty dishes and desserts. Additionally, seasonal ingredients can be highlighted to enhance freshness and appeal. Entrepreneurs should aim to create signature dishes that can establish a strong brand identity and foster customer loyalty. This not only encourages repeat business but also allows for effective marketing opportunities through signature items.

Pricing is a fundamental component of menu development that can significantly impact profitability and customer perception. Entrepreneurs must determine pricing strategies that reflect the quality of ingredients, preparation methods, and overall dining experience. Conducting a competitive analysis to understand what similar businesses charge for comparable items can provide valuable insight. It's crucial to strike a balance between affordability for customers and sustainability for the business. Additionally, incorporating a tiered pricing structure can accommodate different budgets, allowing for a more extensive customer reach while maintaining profit margins.

Transparency in pricing is also essential in building trust with customers. Clearly displaying prices on the menu and being upfront about any additional costs, such as taxes or service charges, can enhance customer satisfaction. Entrepreneurs should consider psychological pricing strategies, such as pricing items just below a round number, to make offerings seem more appealing. Special promotions, happy hour pricing, or bundling options can also encourage higher sales volume, especially during slower periods. By experimenting with various pricing strategies, entrepreneurs can find the most effective approach for their specific market.

Finally, the menu should be dynamic and adaptable. As trends and customer preferences evolve, entrepreneurs must be willing to revise their offerings and pricing accordingly. Regularly soliciting feedback from customers can provide insights into what items are most popular and which may need to be re-evaluated. Seasonal changes can also prompt menu updates, allowing businesses to capitalize on fresh ingredients and current trends. By maintaining a flexible approach to menu development and pricing, entrepreneurs can ensure their side hustle remains relevant and competitive in an ever-changing marketplace.

Food Safety and Compliance Services

Food safety and compliance services are essential for any food-related business aiming to maintain a high standard of quality and ensure public health. Entrepreneurs venturing into the food industry must navigate a complex landscape of regulations, health codes, and safety standards. These services encompass a wide range of activities, including food safety training, compliance audits, and the implementation of food safety management systems. By offering these services, you can help small businesses not only comply with local and federal regulations but also build consumer trust and enhance their reputation in the marketplace.

One of the primary components of food safety services is training staff on proper food handling techniques. Many small food businesses, such as cafes, food trucks, and restaurants, may not have the expertise or resources to conduct thorough training. This gap presents an opportunity for entrepreneurs to develop training programs tailored to the specific needs of these businesses. Courses can cover topics such as safe food storage, cross-contamination prevention, and personal hygiene practices. By equipping employees with the right knowledge, businesses can minimize the risk of foodborne illnesses and ensure compliance with health regulations.

In addition to training, compliance audits are critical in helping food businesses identify potential hazards and rectify them before they become serious issues. Entrepreneurs can offer audit services that evaluate a business's adherence to food safety standards. This process involves reviewing operational practices, inspecting facilities, and assessing documentation related to food safety protocols. By providing detailed reports and actionable recommendations, compliance auditors empower small businesses to make necessary adjustments, ultimately safeguarding their customers and reducing the risk of costly violations.

Another vital aspect of food safety and compliance services is the development and implementation of food safety management systems. These systems help businesses create a structured approach to managing food safety risks. Entrepreneurs can assist small businesses in crafting customized plans that address their unique challenges and operational realities. This may include establishing standard operating procedures, monitoring and verification processes, and documentation practices. A robust food safety management system not only helps in compliance but also fosters a culture of safety and accountability among staff.

As the demand for safe food continues to grow, entrepreneurs can capitalize on the increasing need for food safety compliance services. By positioning themselves as knowledgeable partners in food safety, these individuals can build a sustainable side hustle that supports the success of small businesses. With the right skills and expertise, they can become indispensable assets for food entrepreneurs, ensuring that their operations run smoothly, legally, and safely. This not only benefits the businesses they serve but also contributes to the overall health and well-being of the community.

Delivery and Logistics Solutions

Delivery and logistics solutions are essential components for small businesses striving to meet customer demands efficiently. As e-commerce continues to grow, entrepreneurs have an opportunity to tap into this lucrative sector by offering tailored delivery services. The key lies in understanding the unique needs of various businesses, such as restaurants, retail shops, or e-commerce platforms. Each of these niches requires specific logistics strategies that can enhance their operational efficiency and improve customer satisfaction.

For restaurants, timely delivery is critical. Entrepreneurs can consider providing a service that includes order tracking and real-time updates for customers. This not only enhances customer experience but also reduces the likelihood of missed deliveries. Additionally, offering specialized packaging solutions that maintain food quality during transit can set a delivery service apart from competitors. By focusing on the unique requirements of the food industry, entrepreneurs can create a compelling value proposition that appeals to local eateries.

Retail shops also have distinct logistics needs, particularly in managing inventory and shipping products. A side hustle in this niche could involve developing a logistics platform that allows retailers to easily manage their shipping processes. This could include features like bulk shipping discounts, scheduled pickups, and integration with various e-commerce platforms. By streamlining logistics for retail businesses, entrepreneurs can help them reduce costs and improve their service offerings, leading to increased customer loyalty.

E-commerce platforms represent another significant market for delivery and logistics solutions. As online shopping becomes increasingly common, businesses are constantly seeking ways to enhance their delivery capabilities. Entrepreneurs can explore opportunities in last-mile delivery services, offering faster and more reliable solutions. Creating partnerships with local courier services can expand delivery options and improve service speed, making it easier for e-commerce businesses to meet consumer expectations for quick deliveries.

In summary, the delivery and logistics sector presents a wealth of opportunities for entrepreneurs who are looking for a side hustle that aligns with their interests. By understanding the specific needs of various industries, such as restaurants, retail, and e-commerce, individuals can develop tailored solutions that address common pain points in logistics. This approach not only helps small businesses thrive but also allows entrepreneurs to build a sustainable and profitable business model that supports the ever-evolving landscape of commerce.

Chapter 4: Health and Wellness

Services for Health and Fitness Businesses

Health and fitness businesses thrive on providing effective services that cater to their clients' well-being and goals. As an entrepreneur looking to enter this niche, understanding the specific services that these businesses require can be a key factor in establishing a successful side hustle. From personal training to nutrition consulting, there are numerous avenues through which you can offer valuable support to health and fitness enterprises. Identifying the gaps in the market will allow you to tailor your services to meet the needs of gym owners, fitness studios, and wellness practitioners.

One of the most sought-after services in the health and fitness sector is personal training. Many gyms and studios look for certified trainers to assist their clients in achieving specific fitness goals. Offering your expertise as a freelance personal trainer can provide flexibility while generating income. Additionally, creating online training programs or conducting virtual training sessions can expand your reach beyond local clients. This service not only fulfills the demand for personalized fitness plans but also supports businesses in enhancing their client retention and satisfaction.

Another critical service is nutrition consulting. As clients become increasingly aware of the impact of diet on overall health and fitness, businesses are eager to partner with professionals who can provide dietary guidance. If you have a background in nutrition, offering meal planning services or workshops can be a lucrative side hustle. Health and fitness businesses often seek to incorporate nutrition education into their offerings, making it essential for them to have access to knowledgeable consultants who can provide tailored advice for their clientele.

Marketing services tailored to health and fitness businesses are also in high demand. Many entrepreneurs in this industry struggle to effectively promote their services and attract new clients. If you possess skills in digital marketing, social media management, or content creation, you can offer valuable support. Helping businesses develop engaging marketing strategies that resonate with their target audience can significantly increase their visibility and client base. From crafting compelling social media campaigns to optimizing their websites for search engines, your expertise can become an indispensable asset.

Lastly, administrative support services can be a game changer for health and fitness businesses. Many small gym owners and personal trainers find themselves overwhelmed with the day-to-day operations, from scheduling appointments to managing client records. By offering virtual assistant services, you can help alleviate some of this burden, allowing them to focus more on their clients. This could involve managing bookings, handling customer inquiries, or even assisting with billing and invoicing. Your ability to streamline their operations can enhance their overall efficiency, making it an appealing service for busy entrepreneurs in the health and fitness realm.

Personal Training and Coaching

Personal training and coaching have emerged as significant avenues for entrepreneurs seeking to establish a side hustle. These services cater to a growing market that values health, fitness, personal development, and overall well-being. As people become increasingly aware of the importance of maintaining a healthy lifestyle, the demand for personal trainers and life coaches continues to rise. This trend presents a lucrative opportunity for those who are passionate about fitness and personal development and are looking to monetize their skills.

The personal training niche encompasses a range of services, from one-on-one training sessions to group classes and online coaching. Entrepreneurs can capitalize on this by offering tailored fitness programs that meet the specific needs of their clients. For instance, creating specialized programs for different demographics such as seniors, busy professionals, or athletes can attract diverse clientele. Additionally, offering unique training modalities, such as yoga, Pilates, or strength training, can help differentiate a business in a competitive market.

Coaching, on the other hand, extends beyond physical fitness to include life coaching, career coaching, and wellness coaching. Entrepreneurs can leverage their expertise in a particular area to guide clients toward achieving their personal or professional goals. This could involve providing support in areas such as time management, stress reduction, or business strategy. The flexibility of coaching services allows for various delivery methods, including in-person sessions, virtual meetings, and workshops, making it accessible to a broader audience.

To successfully launch a personal training or coaching business, entrepreneurs should consider obtaining relevant certifications and building a strong personal brand. Certifications not only enhance credibility but also equip trainers and coaches with the necessary skills to deliver effective services. Furthermore, establishing an online presence through social media and a professional website can attract potential clients and showcase expertise. Sharing success stories, testimonials, and informative content can engage an audience and foster trust.

Networking within the fitness and coaching communities is also crucial for growth. Collaborating with gyms, wellness centers, and other professionals can lead to referrals and partnerships. Additionally, attending industry events and workshops can provide valuable insights and trends that can be leveraged to enhance service offerings. By staying informed and connected, entrepreneurs can position themselves as thought leaders in their niche, ultimately driving their side hustle toward success.

Nutrition Consulting

Nutrition consulting is a rapidly expanding field that offers significant opportunities for entrepreneurs interested in health and wellness. As people become increasingly aware of the importance of nutrition to overall health, they seek guidance from professionals who can help them make informed dietary choices. This need for personalized nutrition advice creates a viable side hustle for individuals with a passion for health, diet, and lifestyle improvement. Whether you are a registered dietitian, a health coach, or simply someone with a keen interest in nutrition, this service can be tailored to meet the needs of various clients.

Entrepreneurs entering the nutrition consulting space can focus on several niches, including weight management, sports nutrition, or specialized diets like veganism or gluten-free living. By honing in on a specific area, you can differentiate yourself from competitors and attract a dedicated clientele. For instance, if you have a background in fitness, positioning yourself as a sports nutrition consultant can appeal to athletes and fitness enthusiasts looking to optimize their performance through diet. This targeted approach allows for more effective marketing strategies and service offerings that resonate with your audience.

To establish a successful nutrition consulting business, it is essential to build a strong online presence. This includes creating a professional website, utilizing social media platforms, and engaging with potential clients through informative content such as blogs or webinars. Sharing your expertise through articles on nutrition topics can help position you as an authority in your field, attracting clients who value your knowledge. Additionally, consider offering free initial consultations or workshops to showcase your skills and gain trust within your community.

Networking is another crucial element for success in the nutrition consulting industry. Collaborating with local gyms, wellness centers, and health food stores can open doors to new client referrals. Establishing partnerships with personal trainers or other health professionals can also enhance your service offerings, allowing you to provide comprehensive care to clients. Building relationships within your community not only expands your client base but also fosters a supportive environment for your business to thrive.

As the demand for nutrition consulting continues to grow, entrepreneurs have a unique opportunity to capitalize on this trend. By aligning your services with your personal preferences and expertise, you can create a fulfilling side hustle that not only generates income but also contributes positively to the health and well-being of others. The key to success lies in understanding your target audience, building a strong brand, and continuously engaging with clients to adapt to their evolving needs. Embracing these principles will position you well in a competitive market and help you build a sustainable business.

Wellness Program Development

Wellness program development is an essential aspect for small businesses aiming to foster a healthy work environment and improve employee satisfaction. Entrepreneurs looking to create a side hustle in this niche can capitalize on the growing demand for wellness services. By designing programs tailored to the specific needs of small businesses, you can help them enhance productivity and reduce turnover rates. To effectively develop a wellness program, it is crucial to assess the unique requirements of the business and its employees, which can vary significantly depending on the industry, company size, and workplace culture.

The first step in wellness program development is conducting a needs assessment. This process involves gathering data through surveys, interviews, or focus groups to identify the health and wellness challenges faced by employees. Understanding factors such as stress levels, work-life balance, and existing wellness initiatives will inform the program's design. Entrepreneurs should also consider the demographic makeup of the workforce, as different age groups and lifestyles may require tailored approaches. This foundational step ensures that the wellness program is relevant and aligned with the specific needs of the business.

Once the needs assessment is complete, program developers can outline the key components of the wellness initiative. Effective wellness programs often include physical fitness activities, mental health resources, nutrition education, and work-life balance strategies. Entrepreneurs should consider integrating various services, such as fitness classes, workshops, health screenings, and employee assistance programs. Additionally, leveraging technology through mobile apps or online platforms can enhance accessibility and engagement. By offering a diverse range of services, small businesses can cater to the varied interests and needs of their employees, ultimately leading to higher participation rates.

Communication plays a vital role in the success of any wellness program. Entrepreneurs must ensure that employees are aware of the program's offerings and benefits. This can be achieved through internal marketing strategies, such as newsletters, meetings, or social media updates. Engaging employees through feedback loops can also promote a sense of ownership and investment in the program. By fostering open communication, small businesses can create a culture of wellness where employees feel encouraged to participate and take advantage of available resources.

Finally, evaluating the impact of the wellness program is crucial for ongoing improvement and sustainability. Entrepreneurs should establish metrics to assess the program's effectiveness, such as employee engagement levels, health outcomes, and overall job satisfaction. Regular feedback from participants can provide valuable insights into what is working and what needs adjustment. By continuously refining the wellness program based on this feedback, entrepreneurs can help small businesses maintain a thriving workplace culture that prioritizes employee health and well-being, ultimately contributing to the organization's success.

Chapter 5: Professional Services

Key Services for Consultants and Freelancers

Consultants and freelancers play a crucial role in supporting small businesses, offering specialized skills and services that can drive growth and efficiency. Among the key services they provide, business consulting stands out as a foundational offering. Business consultants help small enterprises identify areas for improvement, streamline operations, and develop strategies for growth. This service often includes market analysis, competitive research, and the creation of actionable business plans. Entrepreneurs looking to start a side hustle in this area should focus on building their expertise in specific industries or business challenges to effectively cater to the needs of their clients.

Another essential service provided by consultants and freelancers is digital marketing. In today's online-driven world, small businesses require robust marketing strategies to reach their target audiences and compete effectively. Services in this niche can include social media management, search engine optimization (SEO), content marketing, and email marketing campaigns. Freelancers with a strong background in digital marketing can help businesses enhance their online presence, increase brand awareness, and drive customer engagement. For entrepreneurs, acquiring skills in digital marketing or partnering with experienced marketers can create a lucrative side hustle opportunity.

Financial consulting is also a vital service that small businesses cannot afford to overlook. Many small business owners lack the expertise to manage their finances effectively or plan for future growth. Freelancers who offer bookkeeping, tax preparation, and financial analysis can provide significant value by helping businesses maintain healthy financial practices. Additionally, financial consultants can assist with budgeting, cash flow management, and investment strategies, ensuring that small businesses are well-equipped to achieve their financial goals. Entrepreneurs with a background in finance can leverage this knowledge to start a rewarding side hustle.

In the realm of technology, IT consulting services are increasingly significant for small businesses. As technology continues to evolve, many small enterprises struggle to keep pace with the latest tools and solutions. IT consultants can offer services such as cybersecurity assessments, software implementation, and system upgrades. By helping businesses navigate the complexities of technology, freelancers can empower their clients to operate more efficiently and securely. Entrepreneurs interested in technology can find ample opportunities in this niche, especially with the growing reliance on digital tools in every aspect of business.

Lastly, training and development services are essential for small businesses aiming to foster employee growth and improve operational efficiency. Freelancers specializing in professional development can provide workshops, coaching sessions, and training programs tailored to the specific needs of a business. These services not only enhance employee skills but also contribute to overall job satisfaction and retention. Entrepreneurs can consider this area as a potential side hustle by leveraging their expertise in a particular field, creating training materials, or offering one-on-one coaching sessions to meet the demands of small businesses striving for continuous improvement.

Branding and Identity Development

Branding and identity development are crucial elements for any entrepreneur looking to establish a side hustle or small business. In an increasingly competitive market, your brand serves as the face of your business, representing not just your products or services but also your values and mission. A well-defined brand identity helps differentiate your offerings from competitors, making it essential for attracting and retaining customers. Entrepreneurs must invest time and effort in creating a brand that resonates with their target audience, as this plays a pivotal role in driving business success.

The first step in branding is defining your unique value proposition. This involves identifying what makes your service distinct and how it fulfills a need within your chosen niche. For instance, if you're considering a side hustle in digital marketing, think about whether you want to focus on social media management, SEO services, or content creation. Each area caters to different client needs and preferences. By pinpointing your niche and articulating your value proposition clearly, you lay the groundwork for a brand that communicates effectively with potential customers.

Once you've established your unique value proposition, the next step is designing your brand identity. This includes creating a memorable logo, selecting a color palette, and developing a consistent visual style that reflects your brand's personality. Your branding elements should work in harmony to create a cohesive image across all platforms, from your website to social media profiles and marketing materials. Consistency is key in building trust and recognition, as consumers are more likely to engage with a brand that presents a unified front.

In addition to visual elements, your brand voice is equally important. This refers to the tone and style of communication you use when interacting with customers, whether through written content, social media posts, or customer service. The voice should align with your target audience's expectations and preferences, helping to forge a deeper connection. For example, a side hustle focused on wellness services might adopt a calm and nurturing tone, while a tech-related service could be more straightforward and innovative. Finding the right voice will enhance your brand identity and foster loyalty among clients.

Finally, ongoing brand management is essential to adapt and grow your identity over time. As market trends shift and customer preferences evolve, your brand should remain relevant and responsive. Regularly soliciting feedback from clients and analyzing industry developments can help inform necessary adjustments to your branding strategy. By maintaining a flexible approach to branding and identity development, entrepreneurs can ensure their side hustle not only survives but thrives in a dynamic business landscape.

Client Management Systems

Client management systems (CMS) are essential tools for entrepreneurs looking to streamline their interactions with clients and improve service delivery. These systems serve as a centralized platform for managing client information, communication, and project tracking, making them invaluable for small businesses. A well-implemented CMS can enhance client relationships, increase efficiency, and ultimately contribute to business growth. For entrepreneurs, understanding how to leverage these systems can be a game-changer in creating a successful side hustle or business.

One of the primary functions of a client management system is to store and organize client data. This includes contact information, communication history, project details, and billing records. By having all relevant information in one place, entrepreneurs can easily access client profiles and tailor their services to meet specific needs. This level of organization not only saves time but also enhances professionalism, as clients appreciate timely and personalized interactions. A CMS can help track client preferences and previous interactions, enabling entrepreneurs to build stronger relationships and foster loyalty.

Communication is another critical aspect of client management, and a CMS can significantly improve this area. Many systems offer integrated communication tools such as email, messaging, and task reminders, which help entrepreneurs stay connected with clients. Automated notifications and follow-ups can ensure that no client feels neglected, while also providing a structured approach to managing multiple projects simultaneously. This consistent communication is vital for small businesses that rely on repeat clients, as it reinforces the importance of client engagement in service-based industries.

Additionally, a CMS can enhance project management capabilities, allowing entrepreneurs to monitor project progress and deadlines effectively. By utilizing features like task assignments, progress tracking, and timeline visualization, small business owners can ensure that projects remain on schedule and within budget. This level of oversight not only helps in managing current client expectations but also aids in forecasting future work and resource allocation. Entrepreneurs can use data from the CMS to analyze performance metrics, which can inform decision-making and strategic planning for growth.

Finally, adopting a client management system can provide valuable insights through reporting and analytics features. These tools can help entrepreneurs understand client behavior, identify trends, and assess service effectiveness. By analyzing this data, small business owners can make informed adjustments to their services, marketing strategies, and pricing models. This adaptability is particularly important in the ever-evolving landscape of small businesses, where staying relevant and responsive to client needs can lead to sustained success. For entrepreneurs exploring their side hustle options, investing in a robust client management system is a critical step in building a business that meets the demands of modern clients.

Financial and Accounting Services

Financial and accounting services are crucial for small businesses, as they form the backbone of sound financial management. Entrepreneurs venturing into side hustles can tap into this niche by offering essential services such as bookkeeping, tax preparation, payroll management, and financial consulting. These services not only help businesses stay compliant with regulations but also enable them to make informed financial decisions. For those looking to start a side hustle, understanding the specific financial needs of small businesses can provide a pathway to success.

One of the primary services entrepreneurs can offer is bookkeeping. Many small business owners struggle with maintaining accurate financial records. This presents an opportunity for side hustlers to provide organized bookkeeping services that can manage day-to-day transactions, reconcile bank statements, and ensure that financial data is up-to-date. By utilizing accounting software, side hustlers can streamline this process, making it efficient and accessible for small business owners who may lack the time or expertise to manage their own finances.

Tax preparation is another area where small businesses often need assistance. Navigating tax laws can be overwhelming, especially for entrepreneurs who may not have a background in finance. Side hustlers can offer tax advisory services to help small business owners maximize deductions, file returns accurately, and plan for future tax liabilities. By staying current with tax regulations and leveraging their knowledge, entrepreneurs can position themselves as trusted advisors, helping small businesses to minimize tax burdens while remaining compliant.

Payroll management is a critical service for small businesses that employ staff. Ensuring employees are paid accurately and on time is essential for maintaining morale and compliance with labor laws. Entrepreneurs can create a side hustle focused on payroll processing, which includes calculating wages, withholding taxes, and managing benefits. By providing this service, side hustlers can alleviate the administrative burden on small business owners, allowing them to focus on growth and operations.

Finally, financial consulting services can offer invaluable insights to small businesses. Entrepreneurs with a strong financial background can provide guidance on budgeting, cash flow management, and strategic planning. This could involve creating financial models, analyzing profitability, and advising on investments or cost reductions. By helping small businesses understand their financial health, side hustlers can foster long-term success and build lasting relationships with clients, positioning themselves as vital partners in their clients' journeys.

Chapter 6: Creative Industries

Supporting Creative Entrepreneurs

Supporting creative entrepreneurs is essential for fostering innovation and growth within various industries. These individuals often possess unique skills and talents that can be transformed into viable business ideas. By understanding the specific needs of creative entrepreneurs, we can create an environment that nurtures their potential and helps them thrive. This subchapter will explore the resources, networks, and strategies available to support these individuals in their journey toward establishing successful side hustles or businesses.

One of the key components in supporting creative entrepreneurs is access to educational resources. Workshops, online courses, and mentorship programs can significantly enhance their skills in areas such as marketing, financial management, and business planning. Many organizations and institutions offer targeted training that focuses on the unique challenges faced by creative professionals. By equipping them with the necessary knowledge and skills, we empower them to make informed decisions and navigate the complexities of running a business, ultimately increasing their chances of success.

Networking plays a critical role in the growth of creative entrepreneurs. Building connections with like-minded individuals, potential collaborators, and industry experts can open doors to new opportunities and resources. Local business organizations, creative meetups, and online platforms can serve as vital hubs for networking. Encouraging creative entrepreneurs to participate in these events can help them establish valuable relationships, gain insights from others in the field, and share their experiences. A strong network can provide emotional support and practical advice, making the entrepreneurial journey less daunting.

Financial support is another crucial aspect of nurturing creative entrepreneurs. Access to funding, whether through grants, loans, or crowdfunding, can significantly impact their ability to launch or expand their businesses. Many financial institutions and organizations now recognize the importance of supporting small businesses and offer tailored programs for creative entrepreneurs. Additionally, teaching them how to create compelling pitches and business plans can enhance their chances of securing funding. Providing financial education and resources will help these entrepreneurs manage their finances effectively and make strategic investments in their ventures.

Lastly, creating a supportive community for creative entrepreneurs can foster a culture of collaboration and innovation. Encouraging events that celebrate local talent, such as art fairs, pop-up shops, or creative markets, can provide a platform for entrepreneurs to showcase their work and connect with potential customers. Additionally, facilitating partnerships between creative entrepreneurs and established businesses can lead to mutually beneficial relationships. By promoting a sense of community and collaboration, we can cultivate an environment where creative entrepreneurs feel valued, supported, and inspired to pursue their passions while contributing to the local economy.

Graphic Design and Branding

Graphic design plays a crucial role in branding, serving as a visual representation of a business's identity and values. For entrepreneurs looking to establish a side hustle, understanding the relationship between graphic design and branding is essential. Every small business needs a cohesive visual identity to differentiate itself in a competitive market. This includes elements such as logos, color schemes, typography, and overall design aesthetics that resonate with the target audience. By offering graphic design services, entrepreneurs can help small businesses create memorable and impactful branding that attracts customers and fosters loyalty.

A strong brand identity goes beyond just a logo; it encapsulates the entire customer experience. Graphic design contributes to this by ensuring that all visual elements align with the brand's message and ethos.

For instance, a tech startup might opt for sleek, modern design elements, while a local bakery might lean towards warm, inviting visuals. Entrepreneurs can tailor their graphic design services to meet the specific needs of different industries, providing personalized solutions that enhance brand recognition. Understanding the nuances of various niches allows graphic designers to create compelling visuals that effectively communicate the essence of each business.

In addition to creating visual identities, graphic design is vital for marketing materials. Small businesses often require brochures, business cards, social media graphics, and promotional content to engage with their audience. Entrepreneurs can tap into this need by offering comprehensive design packages that include both branding and marketing collateral. This not only streamlines the process for small business owners but also ensures consistency across all platforms. A well-designed marketing campaign can significantly impact a business's visibility and customer engagement, making this an appealing service for side-hustling entrepreneurs.

Moreover, the rise of digital platforms has increased the demand for graphic design in online branding. Websites, social media profiles, and digital ads require visually appealing designs that capture attention and convey information quickly. Entrepreneurs who specialize in graphic design can leverage their skills to help small businesses establish a strong online presence. By creating eye-catching social media graphics and website layouts, designers can assist businesses in reaching wider audiences and driving traffic to their services. This growing need for digital design aligns perfectly with the side hustle aspirations of many entrepreneurs.

Finally, as branding trends continue to evolve, staying updated on the latest design techniques and tools is paramount for graphic designers. Entrepreneurs can enhance their side hustle by investing time in learning about emerging design trends, software, and best practices. Networking with other professionals in the field can also provide valuable insights and opportunities for collaboration. By positioning themselves as knowledgeable and versatile graphic designers, entrepreneurs can build a reputation that attracts small businesses in need of branding and design services, ultimately leading to a successful side hustle.

Content Creation and Marketing

Content creation and marketing are vital components for any small business aiming to establish a solid online presence and engage effectively with its target audience. Entrepreneurs looking to start a side hustle in this area should understand that creating valuable, relevant content can significantly enhance brand visibility and customer loyalty. Whether it's through blog posts, videos, social media updates, or newsletters, consistently producing quality content helps businesses communicate their message, showcase their expertise, and connect with potential clients.

To begin with, identifying the specific content needs of small businesses is crucial. Different niches require tailored content strategies. For example, a local restaurant may benefit from mouth-watering food photography and engaging social media posts, while a law firm might focus on informative articles that address common legal questions. Understanding these nuances allows entrepreneurs to craft content that resonates with the target audience and meets the unique demands of each business. Conducting market research and staying updated on industry trends can provide insights into what types of content are most effective.

Once the content needs are identified, developing a content calendar is an effective way to maintain consistency and organization. A well-structured calendar helps businesses plan their content in advance, ensuring that they cover a diverse range of topics while aligning with seasonal events or promotions. This strategic approach not only keeps the audience engaged but also allows businesses to optimize their marketing efforts, as they can analyze the performance of various content types and refine their strategy accordingly.

In addition to creating content, effective marketing strategies are essential to ensure that the content reaches the intended audience. Utilizing social media platforms, email marketing, and search engine optimization (SEO) techniques can significantly boost visibility. Entrepreneurs should consider offering free resources, such as e-books or webinars, to attract leads and build an email list. This not only positions the business as an authority in its field but also provides opportunities for nurturing leads over time.

Finally, measuring the effectiveness of content creation and marketing efforts is vital for ongoing success. Entrepreneurs should utilize analytics tools to track engagement metrics, such as website traffic, social media interactions, and conversion rates. By analyzing this data, small business owners can assess what works and what doesn't, allowing them to refine their content strategies for better results. This iterative process ensures that businesses remain agile and responsive to their audience's needs, ultimately driving growth and sustainability in an increasingly competitive marketplace.

Photography and Videography Services

Photography and videography services have become essential for small businesses looking to enhance their brand presence and engage their audience effectively. In a digital age where visual content dominates social media and online marketing, entrepreneurs can leverage their skills in photography and videography to meet the growing demand from various industries. From product photography for e-commerce sites to promotional videos for local businesses, the opportunities to create compelling visual content are vast and varied. Understanding the specific needs of businesses in your area can help you tailor your services accordingly.

For retail businesses, high-quality product images are crucial. A well-captured photograph can make a significant difference in attracting customers and driving sales. Entrepreneurs can offer services that include studio setups for product shoots, lifestyle photography that showcases products in use, and even 360-degree product views. Additionally, seasonal promotions or special events often require fresh visual content, creating ongoing opportunities for photographers and videographers. By establishing a niche in product photography, you can position yourself as an indispensable partner for local retailers.

Service-based businesses, such as salons, gyms, and restaurants, also benefit from professional photography and videography. For instance, a salon may need before-and-after shots of hairstyles, while a restaurant can use mouth-watering images of its dishes to entice customers. Videography can take this a step further, allowing businesses to share their unique stories through engaging video content. This could include virtual tours, client testimonials, or how-to videos that showcase the expertise of the service provider. Offering tailored packages that cater to these specific needs can set you apart from competitors.

Real estate is another lucrative niche that heavily relies on high-quality visuals. Real estate agents and property managers often seek professional photographers to create stunning images of properties, as well as drone videography to provide aerial views. Timely and appealing visuals can help properties sell faster and at higher prices. By developing a portfolio focused on real estate photography and videography, you can attract agents and agencies looking to enhance their listings and marketing efforts.

Finally, event photography and videography can provide a steady stream of clients for entrepreneurs in this field. From corporate events to weddings, capturing the essence of these moments is invaluable. Businesses hosting events often want professional documentation to promote future endeavors or to preserve memories for their clients. Offering packages that include both photography and videography can appeal to a broad range of clients, making your services a one-stop solution for all their visual content needs. By understanding the demands of various sectors, you can effectively market your photography and videography services to entrepreneurs seeking to elevate their brand image.

Chapter 7: Technology and IT Services

Essential Tech Services for Small Businesses

In the modern business landscape, technology plays a pivotal role in the success and sustainability of small businesses. Entrepreneurs venturing into side hustles should be aware of the essential tech services that can significantly enhance operational efficiency and customer engagement. From cloud computing to digital marketing strategies, understanding these services can help small businesses thrive in a competitive environment.

One of the most critical tech services for small businesses is cloud computing. This technology allows businesses to store, manage, and access data over the internet, rather than relying on local servers. For entrepreneurs, this means lower upfront hardware costs and the flexibility to scale operations as needed. Cloud services also facilitate remote work, enabling teams to collaborate seamlessly, which is particularly useful for businesses with a distributed workforce. Providers like Google Workspace and Microsoft 365 offer tools that can streamline communication and project management, making them indispensable for small operations.

Website development and maintenance is another essential service that small businesses cannot overlook. A professional and user-friendly website is often the first point of contact for potential customers. Entrepreneurs should consider investing in responsive web design, search engine optimization (SEO), and ongoing content updates to attract and retain visitors. Additionally, e-commerce capabilities are crucial for businesses looking to sell products online. Platforms such as Shopify or WooCommerce can empower small business owners to establish a robust online presence and reach a wider audience.

Digital marketing services, including social media management and email marketing, are vital for increasing brand visibility and customer engagement. Entrepreneurs should leverage these platforms to create targeted campaigns that connect with their audience. Social media not only serves as a marketing tool but also as a customer service channel, allowing businesses to respond quickly to inquiries and feedback. Email marketing, on the other hand, remains a powerful way to nurture leads and keep customers informed about promotions or new products. Utilizing analytics to track engagement can help entrepreneurs refine their strategies for better results.

Cybersecurity is an often-overlooked but essential tech service that small businesses must prioritize. As businesses increasingly rely on digital tools, they become more vulnerable to cyber threats. Entrepreneurs should invest in comprehensive cybersecurity measures, including firewalls, antivirus software, and employee training on best practices. This not only protects sensitive data but also builds trust with customers, who are increasingly concerned about how their information is handled. Partnering with cybersecurity firms or utilizing managed security services can provide the necessary expertise and resources to safeguard business operations.

In conclusion, small businesses require a variety of tech services to survive and thrive in today's digital environment. Entrepreneurs exploring side hustles should consider the pivotal roles of cloud computing, website development, digital marketing, and cybersecurity in their business models. By integrating these essential services, small business owners can enhance efficiency, foster customer relationships, and ultimately drive growth in their ventures.

Website Development and Maintenance

Website development and maintenance are critical components for small businesses looking to establish a robust online presence. In today's digital age, having a professionally designed website is not just a luxury; it is a necessity. For entrepreneurs considering a side hustle, offering website development can be a lucrative opportunity. Small businesses require websites that are not only visually appealing but also functional and user-friendly. This includes responsive design, which ensures that the site looks great on all devices, from desktops to smartphones. Entrepreneurs can cater to various niches, from local shops and restaurants to service providers and e-commerce platforms, providing tailored solutions that meet specific industry needs.

Once a website is built, ongoing maintenance becomes essential to keep it running smoothly. Small businesses often lack the technical expertise to manage their websites effectively. This creates a demand for services such as regular updates, security monitoring, and performance optimization. By offering website maintenance as a side hustle, entrepreneurs can establish long-term relationships with clients, ensuring that their websites remain up-to-date and secure against cyber threats. This could include routine backups, plugin updates, and content management, all of which are vital for maintaining the integrity and functionality of a website.

Additionally, search engine optimization (SEO) is an integral part of website development and maintenance that entrepreneurs can capitalize on. Many small businesses struggle to appear in search engine results, which directly impacts their visibility and customer acquisition. By providing SEO services, entrepreneurs can help these businesses improve their rankings and drive organic traffic to their websites. This involves keyword research, content creation, and link-building strategies tailored to the specific market and audience of each business. The combination of development, maintenance, and SEO provides a comprehensive service that small businesses desperately need to thrive in a competitive landscape.

Content creation is another vital service that can be bundled with website development and maintenance. Small businesses often need high-quality content to engage their audience and convey their brand message effectively. This includes blog posts, product descriptions, and multimedia content, all of which enhance user engagement and improve SEO. As an entrepreneur, offering content creation services alongside website development not only adds value to your offerings but also positions you as a one-stop shop for all digital needs. This can significantly increase client satisfaction and retention, leading to more referrals and repeat business.

Finally, entrepreneurs venturing into website development and maintenance should consider the integration of analytics and performance tracking into their services. Small businesses benefit from understanding their website's performance metrics, such as visitor behavior, traffic sources, and conversion rates. By providing insights through tools like Google Analytics, entrepreneurs can help clients make informed decisions about their online strategies. This data-driven approach not only enhances the value of the services offered but also empowers small business owners to optimize their online presence continually. In summary, website development and maintenance represent a significant opportunity for entrepreneurs looking to create a sustainable side hustle while fulfilling the essential needs of small businesses.

Cybersecurity Solutions

Cybersecurity has become an integral part of running a successful small business, particularly in an age where digital transactions and online communications dominate. Entrepreneurs venturing into the realm of side hustles must understand that cybersecurity solutions are not just a luxury but a necessity for safeguarding sensitive information and maintaining customer trust. Small businesses often fall prey to cyber threats due to their limited resources and lack of awareness, making them prime targets for cybercriminals. Therefore, providing cybersecurity services can be a profitable niche for entrepreneurs looking to support small business operations.

One of the fundamental cybersecurity solutions small businesses require is the implementation of robust firewalls. Firewalls act as a barrier between a company's internal network and external threats, monitoring incoming and outgoing traffic to prevent unauthorized access. Entrepreneurs can offer services to assess existing firewall setups, configure them correctly, and provide ongoing monitoring and maintenance. Additionally, educating small business owners on the importance of firewalls and how they function can enhance their understanding and commitment to cybersecurity.

Another critical area is data protection and encryption. Small businesses handle valuable customer data, including payment information and personal identification. Offering data encryption services ensures that sensitive information is converted into unreadable code, making it inaccessible to unauthorized users. Entrepreneurs can provide consultations on data protection policies, assist in implementing encryption software, and develop strategies for regular data backups. By emphasizing the importance of data integrity and compliance with regulations such as GDPR or CCPA, aspiring entrepreneurs can position themselves as indispensable partners for small business owners.

Employee training and awareness programs are also essential components of a comprehensive cybersecurity strategy. Many cyber threats, such as phishing attacks, exploit human vulnerabilities. Entrepreneurs can create training modules tailored to small business needs, focusing on recognizing potential threats and adhering to best practices in cybersecurity. Regular workshops and updates on emerging threats can help foster a culture of security within small businesses, empowering employees to act as the first line of defense against cyber-attacks.

Finally, offering incident response and recovery services can be a valuable addition to a cybersecurity side hustle. In the event of a security breach, small businesses need to act swiftly to mitigate damage and restore operations. Entrepreneurs can provide services that include developing incident response plans, conducting vulnerability assessments, and offering post-incident recovery support. By helping small business owners prepare for potential cyber incidents, entrepreneurs can not only enhance their clients' resilience but also build long-term relationships based on trust and reliability in the rapidly evolving digital landscape.

IT Support and Consulting

IT support and consulting is a crucial service that small businesses rely on to navigate the complexities of technology. As entrepreneurs increasingly integrate digital tools into their operations, the demand for reliable IT support has surged. Small businesses often lack the resources to maintain a full-time IT department, making outsourcing IT support an appealing side hustle. By offering services such as network setup, troubleshooting, software installation, and cybersecurity solutions, aspiring entrepreneurs can position themselves as invaluable partners to local businesses struggling to keep up with technological advancements.

One of the primary needs small businesses face is the maintenance and security of their IT infrastructure. Many entrepreneurs may not have the technical knowledge to manage their systems effectively, leading to vulnerabilities that can be exploited by cybercriminals. Providing IT consulting services allows you to assess a business's current technology, recommend improvements, and implement security measures to protect sensitive data. This not only enhances the client's operational efficiency but also builds trust and credibility in your expertise.

Furthermore, the rapid evolution of technology means that small businesses must stay updated on the latest tools and software to remain competitive. Offering training sessions or workshops can be a valuable addition to your IT support services. This could include teaching employees how to use new software, implementing best practices for data management, or providing guidance on digital marketing tools. By equipping businesses with the knowledge they need, you empower them to make informed decisions that can lead to increased productivity and growth.

Another essential aspect of IT support is troubleshooting and technical assistance. Small businesses often encounter unexpected technical issues that can halt operations and lead to lost revenue. As an IT consultant, you can provide remote or on-site support to quickly resolve these issues. By establishing a reliable support system, you can help businesses minimize downtime and maintain their operational flow. Offering a subscription-based model for ongoing support can create a steady income stream for your side hustle while ensuring your clients have constant access to assistance when they need it most.

Finally, as you build relationships with small business owners, you may discover additional opportunities for services beyond IT support. Many entrepreneurs are looking for advice on technology strategy, digital transformation, or cloud computing solutions. By expanding your skill set and staying informed about the latest trends, you can position yourself as a comprehensive resource for small businesses looking to thrive in a digital landscape. This holistic approach not only enhances your reputation but also increases your potential for referrals, creating a sustainable side hustle that meets the ongoing needs of small businesses.

Chapter 8: Home and Personal Services

Services for Home-Based Businesses

Home-based businesses have gained popularity in recent years, driven by advancements in technology and changing work preferences. Entrepreneurs venturing into this realm often seek services that can enhance their operations and streamline processes. From administrative support to marketing strategies, a comprehensive understanding of the services needed by home-based businesses can provide aspiring entrepreneurs with valuable opportunities for their side hustles.

One essential service for home-based businesses is virtual assistance. Entrepreneurs often juggle multiple responsibilities, from managing customer inquiries to handling administrative tasks. Virtual assistants can help alleviate this burden by managing schedules, responding to emails, and performing data entry tasks. This support allows business owners to focus on their core offerings while ensuring that essential operational functions are maintained. For those looking to start a side hustle, offering virtual assistance can be a straightforward entry point into the world of small business services.

Another critical area where home-based businesses require support is digital marketing. Establishing an online presence is crucial for attracting customers, and many entrepreneurs need help navigating the complexities of social media, search engine optimization, and email marketing. Services such as content creation, social media management, and targeted advertising campaigns can significantly boost visibility and engagement. Entrepreneurs interested in digital marketing can offer specialized services tailored to the unique needs of various home-based businesses, helping them reach their target audience more effectively.

Accounting and financial management services are also vital for home-based entrepreneurs. Many business owners lack the expertise or time to manage their finances properly, leading to potential pitfalls down the line. Services such as bookkeeping, tax preparation, and financial consulting can provide invaluable assistance. Entrepreneurs with a knack for numbers can capitalize on this need by offering tailored financial services, ensuring that home-based businesses maintain healthy financial practices and comply with regulations.

Finally, technology support is an indispensable service for home-based businesses that rely heavily on digital tools. As businesses integrate various software solutions for project management, customer relationship management, and e-commerce, the need for tech support becomes apparent. Entrepreneurs can explore opportunities in providing IT support, software training, or even website design and maintenance services. By addressing the technological challenges faced by home-based businesses, aspiring entrepreneurs can create a niche that not only fulfills a demand but also fosters long-term partnerships with their clients.

Cleaning and Maintenance Services

Cleaning and maintenance services play a vital role in the sustainability and success of small businesses across various industries. Entrepreneurs looking for a side hustle can tap into this essential niche, providing services that range from routine janitorial tasks to specialized maintenance. As businesses strive to maintain a clean and safe environment for employees and customers, the demand for reliable cleaning and maintenance services is ever-present. This creates a lucrative opportunity for individuals who possess organizational skills and a keen eye for detail.

One of the primary services small businesses require is regular cleaning. This includes office cleaning, restroom sanitation, and floor care, which are crucial for maintaining a professional image. Many small enterprises operate on tight budgets and often do not have the resources to hire full-time cleaning staff. By offering flexible cleaning schedules—such as daily, weekly, or bi-weekly services—entrepreneurs can cater to the unique needs of different businesses. This adaptability not only makes the service more appealing but also allows the entrepreneur to build long-term relationships with clients.

In addition to standard cleaning, maintenance services are increasingly important for small businesses. This can encompass a wide range of tasks including minor repairs, landscaping, and emergency cleanup services. By providing maintenance solutions, entrepreneurs can assist businesses in preventing larger issues that might arise from neglect. For instance, regular maintenance checks can help identify potential plumbing problems or electrical issues before they escalate, saving the business time and money. Thus, integrating maintenance into the service offering can significantly enhance the value provided to clients.

Moreover, specialized cleaning services are becoming more sought after, particularly in the wake of heightened health and safety awareness. Industries such as healthcare, food service, and retail have rigorous standards that must be met. Entrepreneurs can establish themselves in these niches by acquiring necessary certifications and training. Offering green cleaning options or using eco-friendly products can also attract businesses that are committed to sustainability. This not only sets the entrepreneur apart from competitors but also addresses the growing consumer demand for environmentally responsible practices.

To successfully launch a cleaning and maintenance service, entrepreneurs should consider their target market and tailor their services accordingly. Networking with local business owners, creating a professional online presence, and utilizing social media for marketing can help in establishing credibility and attracting clients. Understanding the specific needs of various businesses and being responsive to their feedback can foster trust and loyalty. By providing reliable, high-quality services, entrepreneurs can position themselves as indispensable partners in the success of small businesses, ensuring a steady stream of income and the potential for growth.

Landscaping and Lawn Care Solutions

Landscaping and lawn care solutions present a lucrative opportunity for entrepreneurs seeking a side hustle that aligns with their passion for outdoor work and environmental aesthetics. This niche not only allows individuals to engage with nature but also provides essential services that homes and businesses require to maintain their curb appeal and functionality. From basic lawn maintenance to advanced landscaping design, the demand for these services is consistently high, making it an attractive option for those looking to start a small business.

The core services in this industry typically encompass lawn mowing, edging, fertilization, weed control, and pest management. Entrepreneurs can cater to residential clients who desire well-maintained yards as well as commercial properties that need to uphold a professional appearance. Offering a variety of packages can attract different customer segments; for instance, weekly maintenance services appeal to busy homeowners, while seasonal clean-up services are perfect for those who prefer to maintain their lawns themselves but need occasional assistance. By understanding the specific needs of their target audience, entrepreneurs can tailor their service offerings accordingly.

In addition to basic lawn care, there is a growing interest in sustainable landscaping practices. Environmental consciousness among consumers is leading to increased demand for eco-friendly solutions such as xeriscaping, native plant landscaping, and organic lawn care. Entrepreneurs can capitalize on this trend by incorporating sustainable practices into their services, thereby appealing to environmentally-minded clients. Providing education on the benefits of these practices can further enhance customer relationships and establish a business as a leader in responsible landscaping.

Technology also plays a pivotal role in the landscaping and lawn care sector. Entrepreneurs can utilize software for scheduling, invoicing, and customer management, making operations more efficient and streamlined. Moreover, the introduction of smart irrigation systems and landscape design apps allows for innovative service offerings that can set a business apart from competitors. Leveraging technology not only improves service delivery but can also enhance customer experience through personalized communication and transparent service updates.

Finally, networking and building relationships within the community can significantly impact the success of a landscaping and lawn care business. Collaborating with local nurseries, garden centers, and real estate agents can lead to mutual referrals and expanded customer bases. Additionally, participating in community events or workshops can provide visibility and establish credibility within the local market. By fostering strong connections and maintaining a reputation for quality service, entrepreneurs can create a sustainable side hustle that meets the ongoing needs of their clientele.

Personal Concierge and Errand Services

Personal concierge and errand services have emerged as a vital resource for busy individuals and small businesses alike, offering a practical solution to the increasing demands of modern life. As entrepreneurs look for side hustle opportunities, this niche presents a unique avenue to explore. These services cater to clients who need assistance with everyday tasks, enabling them to focus on their core responsibilities. By providing personalized support, entrepreneurs can carve out a profitable niche while fulfilling a genuine need in the market.

The services offered by a personal concierge can vary widely, ranging from simple errands like grocery shopping and dry cleaning pick-up to more complex tasks such as travel planning and event coordination. This flexibility allows entrepreneurs to tailor their offerings based on their skills and interests. For example, someone with a knack for organization might excel in helping clients declutter their homes or manage their schedules, while another person with strong communication skills could thrive in coordinating meetings or handling client relations for small businesses. This adaptability makes personal concierge services an appealing option for many aspiring entrepreneurs.

Targeting specific demographics can further enhance the potential for success in this field. Busy professionals, families, and elderly individuals often require assistance with daily tasks, making them ideal clients. Additionally, small business owners frequently juggle multiple responsibilities and may seek help with administrative duties or project management. By identifying and understanding the needs of these target markets, entrepreneurs can create tailored service packages that meet their clients' specific requirements, thereby increasing their value proposition.

To establish a personal concierge and errand service, entrepreneurs should consider the necessary tools and resources. A well-designed website or social media presence can serve as a platform for marketing services and managing client inquiries. Networking with local businesses, such as real estate agents or event planners, can also facilitate referrals and create mutually beneficial partnerships. Furthermore, developing strong organizational and time management skills will be critical in ensuring that tasks are completed efficiently and to client satisfaction, ultimately leading to repeat business and positive word-of-mouth referrals.

In summary, personal concierge and errand services not only provide a valuable service to clients but also represent an entrepreneurial opportunity that is accessible and adaptable. By leveraging their personal preferences and skills, aspiring entrepreneurs can create a side hustle that aligns with their interests while addressing the needs of a diverse clientele. With a focus on building relationships and delivering exceptional service, those in this field can establish a thriving business that stands out in the competitive landscape of small services.

Chapter 9: Education and Training

Building Educational Services

Building educational services can be a lucrative side hustle for entrepreneurs who possess expertise in a particular subject or skill. This niche is particularly appealing because it allows individuals to share their knowledge while also meeting the growing demand for personalized learning experiences. As more people turn to online platforms for education, the potential for creating a successful educational service business expands significantly. Entrepreneurs can cater to a diverse audience, ranging from school-aged children needing tutoring to adults seeking professional development.

To begin building educational services, entrepreneurs should identify their area of expertise. This could be anything from academic subjects like mathematics and science to practical skills such as coding, graphic design, or even life coaching. Understanding the target market is crucial; entrepreneurs should research the specific needs and challenges faced by their potential clientele. This research will guide the development of tailored educational offerings that resonate with the audience, making the services more appealing and effective.

Next, entrepreneurs can explore various delivery methods for their educational services. Options include one-on-one tutoring, group workshops, online courses, or even creating educational content like eBooks and video tutorials. Each method has its advantages, and entrepreneurs should choose the one that best aligns with their skills and the preferences of their target audience. For instance, online courses can reach a wider audience and offer flexibility, while one-on-one sessions provide personalized attention and support.

Marketing plays a vital role in the success of educational services. Entrepreneurs should leverage social media, online advertising, and word-of-mouth referrals to promote their offerings. Creating a professional website can also enhance credibility and serve as a platform for showcasing testimonials, course descriptions, and pricing information. Engaging with potential clients through informative blogs or free webinars can further establish authority in the field and attract new customers.

Finally, it is essential for entrepreneurs in the educational services sector to continuously assess and improve their offerings. Gathering feedback from clients can provide insights into their experiences and highlight areas for enhancement. Staying updated with the latest trends in education and technology will also help entrepreneurs remain competitive in a rapidly evolving market. By fostering a commitment to quality and adaptability, entrepreneurs can build a sustainable educational service that not only meets the needs of their clients but also aligns with their personal passions and goals.

Tutoring and Mentorship

Tutoring and mentorship present valuable opportunities for entrepreneurs seeking side hustles that align with their skills and interests. With an increasing demand for personalized education and guidance, this niche allows individuals to leverage their expertise while making a meaningful impact on others. Whether you have a background in academics, a specific industry, or life skills, there is a market for your knowledge. Entrepreneurs can identify potential clients such as students, professionals seeking career advancement, or individuals looking to develop new skills.

The tutoring market is diverse, catering to various age groups and subjects. Entrepreneurs can specialize in academic tutoring, providing assistance in subjects such as mathematics, science, or language arts. Alternatively, they can offer test preparation services for standardized exams like the SAT or ACT, where focused training can lead to significant improvements in scores. Moreover, with the rise of online learning platforms, tutoring can easily transition to a virtual format, allowing for flexibility in scheduling and reaching clients beyond local communities.

Mentorship, on the other hand, encompasses a broader scope, focusing on guiding individuals through personal or professional development. Entrepreneurs with experience in specific careers or industries can create mentorship programs tailored to younger professionals or those looking to switch careers. This can include one-on-one coaching sessions, group workshops, or even online courses. By sharing insights and experiences, mentors can help others navigate challenges, set goals, and develop strategies for success, all while building their own brand and potentially generating income.

To effectively market tutoring and mentorship services, entrepreneurs should consider leveraging social media platforms and local community resources. Creating an engaging online presence through social media or a dedicated website can attract potential clients. Additionally, networking within local educational institutions, career centers, or community organizations can provide valuable connections. Offering free workshops or informational sessions can also serve as a promotional tool, showcasing expertise and establishing credibility in the field.

In conclusion, tutoring and mentorship offer entrepreneurs a flexible and rewarding side hustle that can be tailored to their personal strengths and interests. By identifying target markets, developing specialized services, and utilizing effective marketing strategies, individuals can create sustainable businesses that not only provide financial rewards but also contribute to the development and success of others. As the demand for personalized guidance continues to grow, this niche presents a promising opportunity for those looking to make a difference while pursuing their entrepreneurial ambitions.

Online Course Development

Online course development has emerged as a lucrative side hustle for entrepreneurs seeking to leverage their expertise in specific areas. With the increasing demand for online learning, creating and selling courses can be a viable business model that aligns with personal passions and skills. Entrepreneurs can focus on niches such as marketing, finance, health and wellness, or even hobbies like photography and cooking. By tapping into their knowledge and experience, they can provide valuable content that meets the needs of learners seeking to enhance their skills or knowledge in a particular field.

To successfully develop an online course, thorough market research is crucial. Entrepreneurs should identify gaps in the market by analyzing current trends and the types of courses that are popular among learners. This involves understanding the target audience, their pain points, and what solutions they are looking for. By pinpointing these areas, course creators can design content that is not only relevant but also compelling. This process may include surveys, social media engagement, and reviewing existing courses to gather insights into what works and what doesn't.

Once the market is assessed, the next step is to outline the course structure. A well-organized course typically includes modules or sections that progressively build on each other. Each module should have clear learning objectives, ensuring that students know what they will gain from each section. Additionally, incorporating various teaching methods—such as video lectures, quizzes, and interactive assignments—can enhance the learning experience. Entrepreneurs should also consider the length of the course, as excessively long courses may discourage participation while too short ones might not provide enough depth.

After the course content is developed, the next phase involves selecting the right platform for hosting the course. Various online learning platforms, such as Teachable, Udemy, and Thinkific, offer entrepreneurs the tools needed to create, market, and sell their courses. Each platform has its own set of features, pricing structures, and audience reach, making it essential for entrepreneurs to choose one that aligns with their business goals. Additionally, effective marketing strategies, including social media promotion, email marketing, and partnerships with influencers in the niche, can significantly boost visibility and enrollment.

Finally, ongoing course improvement is vital for long-term success. Gathering feedback from students through surveys or direct communication helps identify areas for enhancement. Entrepreneurs should also stay updated with industry trends to ensure that their course content remains relevant. Regularly refreshing the course material and adding new resources can attract repeat customers and encourage referrals. By focusing on continuous improvement and adapting to the evolving needs of learners, entrepreneurs can build a sustainable online course business that not only provides a source of income but also contributes positively to the learning community.

Corporate Training Programs

Corporate training programs have become a critical component for businesses seeking to enhance employee skills, improve productivity, and maintain a competitive edge. These programs can range from onboarding new hires to specialized training sessions tailored to specific roles within the company.

Entrepreneurs looking for a side hustle can tap into this growing demand by offering customized training solutions. By identifying the unique needs of different businesses, entrepreneurs can create targeted programs that address gaps in knowledge and skills, making them valuable partners in the corporate landscape.

One of the key areas where corporate training programs are essential is in compliance and regulatory training. Many industries are subject to stringent regulations, and companies must ensure their employees are well-versed in these requirements. Entrepreneurs can develop training modules that cover compliance topics, such as workplace safety, data protection, or industry-specific regulations. By providing companies with the tools they need to keep their employees informed and compliant, entrepreneurs can establish themselves as trusted resources in a niche that is often overlooked.

Another lucrative area for corporate training is leadership and management development. As organizations grow, the need for effective leadership becomes increasingly important. Entrepreneurs can design programs that focus on developing soft skills, such as communication, conflict resolution, and team-building, alongside hard skills like project management and strategic planning. By offering workshops or coaching sessions tailored to emerging leaders, entrepreneurs can help companies cultivate their talent while simultaneously building a sustainable side hustle.

Technology training is also a significant component of corporate training programs. As businesses increasingly rely on digital tools and platforms, employees must be proficient in using these technologies to maximize efficiency and productivity. Entrepreneurs can create training sessions that cover software applications, data analysis tools, and digital marketing strategies. By staying updated on the latest technological trends, entrepreneurs can provide relevant and timely training that helps businesses adapt to rapidly changing environments.

Lastly, the rise of remote work has created new opportunities for corporate training programs. With many companies shifting to hybrid or fully remote models, the demand for virtual training solutions has surged. Entrepreneurs can leverage online platforms to deliver engaging and interactive training experiences that accommodate various learning styles. By developing a range of resources, from webinars to e-learning courses, entrepreneurs can cater to businesses looking to enhance their workforce's skills without the constraints of traditional training methods. This adaptability not only meets the current market need but also positions entrepreneurs as innovative leaders in the corporate training space.

Chapter 10: List Of Businesses and Services They Need

Small Business Type Essential Services Needed

Do you have a passion and/or ability to provide any of these services to small businesses. If yes you will be able to provide something of value that these businesses need. You may be able to target more than one type of business because your ability may be required by more than one.

For example, if your expertise is IT you can go into small businesses and offer an office maintenance package. Say once a week you will make sure the printers are updated, servers are optimal, internet is optimized etc.

Insurance Companies

- IT support for client management systems

- Document shredding and secure storage solutions

- Marketing materials creation (flyers, ads)

- Compliance and auditing support

- Office furniture and equipment servicing

Bars

- Beer line cleaning and maintenance

- Ice machine repairs and servicing

- POS system installation and upgrades

- Glassware supply and polishing services

- Sound system calibration and maintenance

Animal Removal

- Wildlife exclusion service (sealing entry points)

- Humane trapping and relocation

- Cleanup and sanitation after removal

- Preventative pest proofing solutions

- Nest removal (birds, bees, etc.)

HVAC Companies

- Duct cleaning and sealing

- Refrigerant recovery and recycling

- Filter supply services for commercial systems

- Tool calibration for specialized diagnostics

- Training and certification courses for staff

Appliance Repair

- Replacement part sourcing

- Refrigerant disposal for old appliances

- Vehicle maintenance for service calls

- Online booking and scheduling systems

- Customer follow-up and review management

Remodeling Companies

- Waste and debris removal services

- 3D design and rendering software

- Tool repair and replacement

- Portable restroom rentals for work sites

- Permitting and licensing assistance

Blinds & Shutters

- Custom design and measurement services

- Installation training for new staff

- Motorized blind repair

- Window cleaning for showrooms

- Sample set creation and delivery

Carpet Cleaning

- Equipment maintenance and repairs (steamers, extractors)

- Training in stain and odor removal techniques

- Chemical and detergent delivery

- Water damage restoration partnerships

- Customer scheduling and routing software

Chimney & Fireplace Services

- Chimney sweep brush and tool repairs

- Masonry restoration and sealing services

- Gas fireplace inspection and servicing

- Compliance checks for fire codes

- Specialized vacuum systems for soot removal

Closet & Garage Organizers

- Custom shelving and storage unit manufacturing

- Installation training for modular systems

- Marketing materials for new home builders

- Tool maintenance for precision cuts

- Inventory management for product lines

Concrete Flat Work

- Concrete delivery and pouring

- Equipment rentals (mixers, floats, etc.)

- Surface finishing supplies (polishers, sealants)

- Crack repair and joint sealing services

- Safety equipment and compliance training

Concrete Foundations

- Excavation equipment rentals

- Reinforcement bar (rebar) supply and cutting

- Concrete pump truck maintenance

- Waterproofing and drainage solutions

- Waste and debris hauling

Deck Builders

- Wood supply and delivery (specialized treated lumber)

- Stain and sealant application tools

- Structural inspection services

- Fastener supply (screws, nails, anchors)

- Power tool repairs and calibration

Door & Window Installers

- Glass cutting and repair services

- Weatherproofing supplies and installation

- Motorized and smart door installation training

- Recycling old windows and doors

- Mobile tools for on-site adjustments

Drain & Sewer Cleaners

- Camera inspection tool maintenance

- Hydro jetting equipment servicing

- Chemical delivery for cleaning stubborn clogs

- Emergency plumbing partnerships

- Waste disposal and transport services

Duct Cleaning

- Air duct camera inspections

- Specialized cleaning tools (brushes, vacuums)

- Anti-microbial treatment supplies

- HVAC filter replacement services

- Marketing services for residential outreach

Landscaping Companies

- Equipment maintenance and blade sharpening

- Vehicle and trailer repairs

- Irrigation system installation and repair

- Soil testing and pest control services

Pizzerias

- Commercial mixer maintenance and repairs

- Pizza oven cleaning and calibration

- Refrigeration system servicing

- Grease trap cleaning

Bakeries

- Dough sheeter and mixer repairs

- Oven maintenance and cleaning

- Pest control services

- Bulk ingredient delivery services

Auto Repair Shops

- Lift and alignment machine servicing

- Hazardous waste removal

- Air compressor maintenance

- Uniform cleaning and rental

Hair Salons & Barbershops

- Hair clipper and scissor sharpening

- Salon chair repair and maintenance

- Ventilation and HVAC servicing

- Towel cleaning and sterilization

Restaurants

- Hood vent cleaning and fire system inspections

- POS (Point of Sale) system setup and maintenance

- Deep cleaning of kitchen equipment

- Health code compliance inspections

Construction Companies

- Tool and heavy equipment rentals

- Safety training and certification

- Dumpster rental and waste removal

- Fuel delivery services

Gyms & Fitness Centers

- Equipment repairs and maintenance

- HVAC system servicing

- Sanitization and deep cleaning services

- Locker and shower area maintenance

Pet Grooming Businesses

- Grooming tool sharpening

- Dryer and vacuum repairs

- Pest control and flea prevention

- Specialty pet product supply

Boutiques & Retail Stores

- Display and fixture installation

- Security system installation and monitoring

- Inventory management software setup

- Window cleaning services

Cleaning Companies

- Equipment maintenance for vacuums and scrubbers

- Bulk cleaning supply delivery

- Hazardous material disposal

- Vehicle cleaning and upkeep

Daycares

- Playground equipment inspection and repair

- Carpet and upholstery cleaning

- First aid kit replenishment

- Pest control

Event Planners

- Tent and equipment rentals

- Floral arrangement services

- Custom signage and printing

- Transportation coordination

Farmers

- Tractor and machinery repair

- Irrigation and water pump maintenance

- Seed and soil quality testing

- Fencing installation and repair

Truck Fleets

- Diesel engine repair and maintenance

- Tire replacement and alignment

- Fleet management software services

- Logistics and routing optimization

Home Repair Services

- Tool sharpening and calibration

- Vehicle and trailer maintenance

- Safety equipment certification

- Advertising and lead generation services

Florists

- Refrigeration system maintenance for flower storage

- Floral delivery services

- Bouquet and arrangement supplies

- Waste disposal for organic materials

Photographers

- Camera and lens cleaning and repairs

- Studio lighting and backdrop setup services

- Photo editing and printing services

- Website and portfolio hosting

Mobile Food Vendors

- Food truck maintenance and repair

- Propane refills and inspections

- Commissary kitchen rentals

- Permit and licensing assistance

Independent Coffee Shops

- Espresso machine maintenance and repairs

- Water filtration system servicing

- POS (Point of Sale) system support

- Barista training and certification

Specialty Retail Stores

- Inventory management solutions

- Customized shelving and display installation

- Branding and signage design

- E-commerce integration services

Tailors & Alteration Shops

- Sewing machine maintenance and repairs

- Fabric supply sourcing

- Specialty cleaning services

- Pattern design software training

Small Farms

- Crop protection and pest control services

- Greenhouse installation and maintenance

- Equipment rental for planting and harvesting

- Soil nutrient analysis

- Maintenance and upkeep of animals and equipment.

Artisan & Craft Businesses

- Tool sharpening for woodworking or metalworking tools

- 3D printer maintenance for modern crafts

- Packaging and shipping solutions

- Social media marketing services

Medical Offices

- Medical equipment calibration and maintenance

- Document shredding and disposal services

- Waiting room furniture cleaning and repairs

- IT and patient record management software

Laundromats

- Washer and dryer repair services

- Coin or card-operated payment system servicing

- Vending machine restocking

- Floor drain and plumbing maintenance

Bed and Breakfasts

- Linen cleaning and supply services

- Appliance maintenance for kitchens and guest rooms

- Landscaping and exterior property upkeep

- Marketing and listing optimization for booking platforms

Pet Boarding & Daycare

- Kennel and cage cleaning and repairs

- Pet grooming and bathing supplies

- Pest control for fleas and ticks

- Staff training in animal behavior and safety

Handyman Businesses

- Tool sharpening and calibration

- Work vehicle maintenance

- Marketing and client management software

- Safety equipment rentals and certifications

Car Washes

- Pressure washer repair

- Soap and chemical supply

- Wastewater management and filtration

- Vacuum system maintenance

Tech Repair Shops

- Replacement parts sourcing

- Specialized equipment calibration

- Software updates and licensing

- IT security training

Specialty Grocery Stores

- Refrigeration and freezer maintenance

- Custom signage and labeling

- Pest control services

- Shelf stocking and product rotation services

Taxi and Rideshare Drivers

- Vehicle detailing and sanitization

- GPS and app integration

- Tire and brake maintenance

- Insurance and licensing support

Independent Mechanics

- Diagnostic tool calibration

- Specialty tool rentals

- Waste oil and hazardous material disposal

- Advertising and lead generation

Wedding Planners

- Venue sourcing and coordination

- Custom decorations and rentals

- Event cleanup services

- Vendor management systems

Independent Bookstores

- Custom shelving and display solutions

- Website setup for online sales

- Book repair and restoration services

- Inventory management software

Microbreweries

- Keg cleaning and maintenance

- Equipment calibration for brewing tanks

- Bottling and labeling services

- Wastewater and byproduct management

Dry Cleaners

- Press and steamer maintenance

- Delivery and pickup route planning

- Solvent recycling and disposal

- Uniform cleaning and repairs

Farmers Markets Vendors

- Tent and stall rentals

- Point-of-sale (POS) system setup

- Product packaging design and printing

- Food safety certification

Tattoo Studios

- Autoclave sterilizer maintenance

- Specialized ink and supply delivery

- Tattoo gun repair and calibration

- Lighting and workstation setup

Independent Tutors

- Virtual learning platform setup

- Marketing services for lead generation

- Learning material printing and design

- Scheduling and payment system integration

Mobile Car Detailers

- Waterless washing solutions

- Power tool and extractor maintenance

- High-quality cleaning product delivery

- Vehicle wrap advertising

Specialty Repair Shops

- Tool calibration and maintenance

- Niche part sourcing

- Waste disposal services for old materials

- Website for online appointment booking

Independent Caterers

- Portable kitchen equipment rentals

- Food transportation solutions

- Health and safety certification

- Custom menu printing services

Coworking Spaces

- IT infrastructure maintenance

- HVAC system servicing

- Coffee machine and kitchen appliance upkeep

- Interior design and furniture sourcing

Mobile Mechanics

- Specialized diagnostic equipment servicing

- Portable tool kits for specific vehicle types

- Waste material disposal for roadside repairs

- Advertising on local apps and platforms

Vintage Clothing Stores

- Clothing repair and restoration services

- Custom tagging and labeling solutions

- Storefront window and display cleaning

- E-commerce platform integration

Dog Walking & Pet Sitting

- Scheduling and route optimization apps

- First aid training for pets

- Collars, leashes, and other pet equipment supply

- Liability insurance assistance

Small Home-Based Bakers

- Oven and kitchen equipment servicing

- Bulk ingredient delivery

- Packaging design and sourcing

- Compliance with local food safety laws

Bike Shops

- Bicycle assembly and repair training

- Specialized tool calibration

- E-bike battery recycling

- Retail POS system integration

Chapter 11: Conclusion and Next Steps

Evaluating Your Side Hustle Options

Evaluating your side hustle options is crucial for entrepreneurs seeking to align their business endeavors with personal interests and market demands. The first step in this evaluation process is to conduct a self-assessment to identify your skills, passions, and resources. What are you good at? What do you enjoy doing? Understanding your strengths allows you to pinpoint which side hustles will not only be sustainable but also enjoyable. This reflection can help you create a list of potential side hustle ideas that resonate with your personal preferences and expertise.

Once you have a list of potential side hustles, the next step is to research the market demand for each option. Investigate local and online marketplaces to see what services are currently in demand and how they align with your interests. Look at trends within your community and broader economic indicators. This research can involve analyzing competitors, exploring customer reviews, and identifying service gaps. By understanding what small businesses need to survive, you can tailor your side hustle to meet those specific demands, increasing your chances of success.

After establishing demand, consider the scalability and sustainability of your chosen side hustle ideas. Assess the potential for growth within each option. Some services may start small but have the potential to expand significantly. For instance, freelance graphic design may begin as a part-time gig but could evolve into a full-service agency with time. Evaluate what resources, time, and effort each side hustle will require to sustain it over the long term. A side hustle that can grow with your ambitions can provide a more fulfilling entrepreneurial journey.

Additionally, think about the financial implications of your potential side hustles. Estimate the initial investment needed for each option and the expected return on investment. Some side hustles, like consulting or tutoring, may require minimal upfront costs, while others, such as launching a product line, could be capital-intensive. Create a budget and a financial plan that accounts for not only startup costs but also ongoing expenses and pricing strategies. Understanding your financial commitment will help you make informed decisions about which side hustle to pursue.

Finally, consider your personal lifestyle and commitments when evaluating side hustle options. Your available time, family responsibilities, and existing job commitments will all influence which side hustles are feasible. Choose a side hustle that fits well into your current schedule and allows for a balanced life. The right side hustle should not only align with your entrepreneurial goals but also enhance your overall well-being. By carefully evaluating your options, you can select a side hustle that is not only viable but also enriching on both personal and professional levels.

Creating a Business Plan

Creating a business plan is a crucial step for entrepreneurs looking to establish a successful side hustle. A well-structured business plan serves as a roadmap, guiding you through the initial phases of your venture and helping you navigate challenges along the way. This document should articulate your business goals, outline your strategies for achieving them, and provide a clear understanding of your target market. By crafting this plan, you will not only clarify your own vision but also create a tool that can attract potential investors or partners.

The first component of a solid business plan is an executive summary. This section provides a brief overview of your business concept, including the services you intend to offer and the unique value proposition that sets you apart from competitors. Define your niche clearly and explain how your side hustle aligns with your personal preferences and skills. This is your opportunity to capture the essence of your business while demonstrating your passion and commitment to prospective stakeholders.

Next, conduct thorough market research to understand the demand for your services within your chosen niche. Identify your target audience, paying attention to demographics, preferences, and pain points. Analyze competitors to understand their strengths and weaknesses, which can help you carve out your market position. This research will not only help you refine your service offerings but also inform your marketing strategies, ensuring that you effectively reach those who will benefit from what you provide.

Financial planning is another critical element of your business plan. Create detailed projections for your startup costs, ongoing expenses, and potential revenue streams. This financial framework will help you assess the feasibility of your business idea and identify funding sources if necessary. Include break-even analysis and cash flow forecasting to ensure that you can sustain your side hustle in the long run. Understanding your financial landscape will empower you to make informed decisions as you grow your business.

Finally, outline your operational plan, which details how you will run your business on a day-to-day basis. This includes processes for delivering your services, managing customer relationships, and handling administrative tasks. Establishing clear operational procedures will enhance your efficiency and allow you to focus on scaling your business. Additionally, consider how you will evaluate your progress and adapt your strategies over time. A flexible approach will enable you to respond to market changes and continuously improve your offerings, ensuring your side hustle remains relevant and successful.

Networking and Building Connections

Networking and building connections are integral components of establishing a successful side hustle. For entrepreneurs looking to create a business that aligns with their personal preferences, developing a robust network can provide invaluable resources, knowledge, and opportunities. The relationships you cultivate can lead to partnerships, referrals, and insights that can help you navigate the complexities of launching and maintaining a small business. Understanding how to effectively network can set the foundation for your entrepreneurial journey.

One of the first steps in building connections is identifying your target audience and potential partners within your chosen niche. Conducting thorough research on small businesses and the services they require will help you understand where your skills and offerings can fill gaps. For instance, if you are interested in providing marketing services, connect with local retailers who may need assistance in promoting their products. Attend events, workshops, and meetups where small business owners congregate, and engage in discussions that highlight your expertise and willingness to help.

Social media platforms, particularly LinkedIn, offer a modern avenue for networking with potential clients and collaborators. By creating a strong online presence, you can showcase your skills and services while interacting with other entrepreneurs. Sharing relevant content, commenting on industry trends, and participating in groups can increase your visibility and establish you as a knowledgeable resource in your field. Online networking is not just about self-promotion; it's about building genuine relationships that can lead to mutual support and collaboration.

In-person networking, while sometimes overlooked in the digital age, remains a powerful tool for establishing connections. Local business associations, chambers of commerce, and industry-specific gatherings can provide face-to-face opportunities to meet potential clients and partners. Prepare an elevator pitch that succinctly conveys who you are and what you offer. Being approachable and authentic can foster trust and open doors to conversations that may evolve into fruitful business relationships.

Finally, nurturing your network is as important as building it. Regular follow-ups, sharing resources, and offering assistance to your connections can strengthen your relationships over time. Consider setting up informal coffee meetings or virtual catch-ups to maintain contact. By demonstrating your commitment to helping others succeed, you position yourself as a valuable ally in your network. This reciprocity can lead to referrals and opportunities that align with your side hustle ambitions, ultimately contributing to the sustainability and growth of your small business.

Taking Action: Launching Your Side Hustle

Launching a side hustle requires careful planning and decisive action. First, identify your skills and interests. This self-assessment not only helps you choose a business that aligns with your passions but also ensures that you are more likely to stay committed during challenging times. Consider what services are in demand within your community or industry. Research local small businesses to understand their needs and the gaps in the market. By aligning your strengths with these demands, you can carve out a niche that suits both your expertise and the needs of potential clients.

Once you have a clear idea of your side hustle, the next step is to create a business plan. This plan should outline your objectives, target audience, pricing structure, and marketing strategies. Define what services you will offer and how they will benefit your clients. Establishing a solid foundation will not only guide your actions but will also make it easier to secure potential clients or investors. A well-thought-out business plan acts as a roadmap, helping you navigate the initial stages of your side hustle and keeping you focused on your goals.

Next, it's time to establish your brand and online presence. In today's digital world, having a professional website and active social media profiles is crucial. Your website should clearly communicate your services, showcase testimonials, and provide easy access for potential customers to contact you. Social media platforms can be leveraged to engage with your audience and promote your services. Creating content that highlights your expertise can attract potential clients and establish your authority in your niche. Consistency in branding and messaging across all platforms will help build trust and recognition among your target audience.

Networking plays a critical role in launching your side hustle. Attend local business events, workshops, and meetups to connect with other entrepreneurs and potential clients. Building relationships within your community can lead to referrals and collaborations that benefit your business. Don't hesitate to reach out to existing contacts, as they may offer valuable insights or opportunities. Additionally, consider joining online communities or forums related to your niche, where you can share knowledge, ask questions, and gain support from like-minded individuals.

Finally, take the leap and start offering your services. Start small, and be prepared to adapt as you learn from your experiences. Collect feedback from your initial clients to improve your offerings and customer service. Establishing a reputation for delivering quality work will lead to repeat business and referrals. As your side hustle grows, remain open to new ideas and opportunities for expansion. By taking action and remaining dedicated to your vision, you can successfully launch a side hustle that not only meets your personal preferences but also fulfills the essential needs of small businesses in your area.

www.ingramcontent.com/pod-product-compliance
Lightning Source LLC
Chambersburg PA
CBHW082256220526
45469CB00009B/3029